RAINBOW WORLD

Senior Authors
Carl B. Smith
Virginia A. Arnold

Linguistics Consultant
Ronald Wardhaugh

Macmillan Publishing Co., Inc.
New York
Collier Macmillan Publishers
London

Copyright © 1983 Macmillan Publishing Co., Inc.

All rights reserved. No part of this book may be reproduced or transmitted in any form or by any means, electronic or mechanical, including photocopying, recording, or by any information storage and retrieval system, without permission in writing from the Publisher.

This work is also published in individual volumes under the titles: *Colors* and *Being Me,* copyright © 1983 Macmillan Publishing Co., Inc. Parts of this work were published in earlier editions of SERIES r.

Macmillan Publishing Co., Inc.
866 Third Avenue, New York, New York 10022
Collier Macmillan Canada, Inc.

Printed in the United States of America
ISBN 0-02-131720-8
9 8 7 6 5 4

ACKNOWLEDGMENTS

The publisher gratefully acknowledges permission to reprint the following copyrighted material:

"A Baby for Nicky," from *Nicky's Sister* by Barbara Brenner. Copyright © 1966 by Barbara Brenner. Adapted by permission of Alfred A. Knopf, Inc.

"Brother," from *Hello and Good-by* by Mary Ann Hoberman. Copyright © 1959 by Mary Ann Hoberman. Reprinted by permission of Russell & Volkening, agents for the author.

"Colors Laugh," "Red," "Blue," and "Yellow," from *Hailstones and Halibut Bones* by Mary O'Neill. Copyright © 1961 by Mary LeDuc O'Neill. Reprinted by permission of Doubleday & Company, Inc., and World's Work, Ltd.

"Just Awful," from *Just Awful* by Alma Marshak Whitney. Copyright © 1971 by Alma Marshak Whitney. Reprinted by permission of Addison-Wesley Publishing Company and World's Work, Ltd.

"Little Blue and Little Yellow," from *Little Blue and Little Yellow* by Leo Lionni. Copyright © 1959 by Leo Lionni. Reprinted by permission of Astor-Honor, Inc.

"Look What I Have!" from *A Rumbudgin of Nonsense* by Arnold Spilka. Copyright © 1970 by Arnold Spilka. Reprinted by permission of Charles Scribner's Sons.

"Okay Everybody," from *Near the Window Tree: Poems and Notes by Karla Kuskin.* Copyright © 1975 by Karla Kuskin. By permission of Harper & Row, Publishers, Inc.

"A Present for the Queen," adapted from *How Big Is A Foot?* by Rolf Myller. Copyright © 1962 by Rolf Myller. Used by permission of Atheneum Publishers and Pergamon Press, Ltd.

"This Is My Rock," from *Every Time I Climb A Tree* by David McCord. Copyright © 1967 by David McCord. Reprinted by permission of Little, Brown and Co. Used also by permission of George G. Harrap & Co., Ltd.

"Uncle Harry," adapted from Elizabeth Shub's translation of *Uncle Harry* by Gerlinde Schneider. Copyright © 1972 by Macmillan Publishing Co., Inc. © 1971 Verlag Heinrich Ellerman, München. Used by permission of Macmillan Publishing Co., Inc. and Hamish Hamilton Children's Books, Ltd.

"You, whose day it is . . ." (also entitled "Send Us a Rainbow"), from p. 285 of *Smithsonian Institution BAE Bul. 124, Nootka and Quileute Music,* 1939, by Frances Densmore. By permission of the Smithsonian Institution Press, Smithsonian Institution, Washington, D.C.

Illustrations: Angela Adams, Ray Cruz, Dan Dickas, Blair Drawson, Alfred Fisher, Betty Fraser, Shelly Freshman, Jackie Geyer, Les Gray, Kent Hendrickson, Vladimir & Eva Hervert, Tim & Greg Hildenbrandt, Robert Jackson, Bernie Karlin, Gordon Kibbee, Leo Lionni, Carl Molno, Sal Murdocca, Cynthia Pickard, David Row, Lynn Uhde, Susan Vaeth, Deborah Whitehouse. **Photographs:** James H. Carmichael (Bruce Coleman, Inc.), Jeff Foote (Bruce Coleman, Inc.), Milton Heiberg, Eva Hervert, Sigred Owen, Norman Snyder, Peter Ward (Bruce Coleman, Inc.).

Contents

Introduction to COLORS 9

Colors Laugh, a poem by Mary O'Neill 10

Rico and the Red Pony, a story by Dina Anastasio
    The Flower Shop 12
    Just One Ride 18
    Rico Pretends 24

Red, a poem by Mary O'Neill 30

SKILLS: Words That Go Together
    (Classifying Nouns) 32

Little Blue and Little Yellow, a story by Leo Leonni 34

Blue, a poem by Mary O'Neill 44

SKILLS: Think of the Sound (Long Vowels) 46

A Baby for Nicky, a story by Barbara Brenner
    The Baby in the House 48
    A Sister for Nicky 54

Brother, a poem by Mary Ann Hoberman 62

SKILLS **Find the Letter** (Consonants) **64**

The Fall Leaves, a story by Dina Anastasio
   Why the Leaves Come Down **66**
   The Last Leaves **71**

Yellow, a poem by Mary O'Neill **76**

The Cat Came Back, a ballad **78**

SKILLS **Words Work Together**
   (Compound Words) **86**

A Present for the Queen, a modern folktale,
   (adapted from *How Big Is a Foot?*)
   What Will I Give the Queen? **88**
   How Big Is a Bed? **93**
   How Big Is a Foot? **98**

The Princess and the Pea, a play
   How Can You Tell? **106**
   A Real Princess **112**

SKILLS **What Is the Big Idea?** (Main Idea) **118**

Conclusion for COLORS **120**

Introduction to BEING ME 121

Okay Everybody, a poem by Karla Kuskin 122

Never Great, a story by Elizabeth Levy
   Not Bad 124
   New Boy in School 128

This Is My Rock, a poem by David McCord 134

SKILLS: Make Opposites (Antonyms) 136

The Song of Little Frog, a story by George Richards
   Frogs Don't Sing 138
   At Old Frog's House 143
   What Little Frog Did 149

Sing Along, four poems by Joyce Kennedy 158

SKILLS: Why? (Drawing Conclusions) 160

Uncle Harry, a story by Gerlinde Schneider
   No Room for a Kitten 162
   A Home for Minx 170

SKILLS: Use a Map (Map Reading) 174

Little Leroy, *a story by George McCue*
    Time to Eat **176**
    Where Is Leroy? **181**

The School of Fish, *a poem by Alma Whitney* **186**

In the Water, *an article by Sally R. Bell* **188**

SKILLS: Find the Sounds (Diphthongs) **194**

Betsy, *a story by Alma Whitney*
    A Very Good Girl **196**
    Time for Bed **200**
    Beets for Breakfast **204**

Look What I Have! *a poem by Arnold Spilka* **212**

Just Awful, *a story by Alma Whitney*
    How Do You Feel? **214**
    The Three-Part Treatment **221**

You, Whose Day It Is, *an American-Indian poem*
    by Nootka **228**

SKILLS: Pick the Letters (Consonant Digraphs) **230**

Conclusion for BEING ME **232**

Word List **233**

COLORS

Colors are a part of the way you live.
They are part of what you see
and what you think.
What color do you like?
Is there a color you don't like?

When you read "Colors,"
you will read about a red pony.
As you read, look for things
with other colors, too.

COLORS LAUGH

Colors laugh
And colors cry—
Turn off the light
And colors die.

And you and you and I
Know well
Each has a taste
Each has a smell
And each has a wonderful
Story to tell...

— Mary O'Neill

11

RICO and the RED PONY

Dina Anastasio

Part One
The Flower Shop

Rico lived in a big city.
And he ran a flower shop.
Rico loved his flowers,
for the flowers were very quiet.
And Rico loved quiet.

But the city where Rico lived
was not quiet.

If he saw a car or bus, Rico yelled,
"Quiet! Why can't you be quiet?"

Then he said to himself,
"Rico, you don't like this city.
Why don't you move away?"

But Rico didn't move out of the city.

At the flower shop there was
a little red pony.
Rico did not like this pony.
But the boys and girls loved it.
Every day they came to the shop.
They jumped on the pony,
and they put in money.
The little red pony went
up and down.
As the pony went up and down,
the children liked to pretend.

They liked to pretend that
they were in the country.

They yelled, "Look at me, look at me!"
Or "Go, pony, go!"

And they were happy.

But they were not quiet.
And that is why Rico
did not like the pony.
Every day he came out of his shop
and yelled at the children.

"**Quiet!**" he said to them.
"**Why can't you be quiet?**"

Rico yelled at them,
and the children ran away.

But they came back.
They came back every day.
And every day Rico yelled at them.

Part Two
Just One Ride

One day Rico came out of his shop.
He looked at the boys and girls.
He thought and thought.
Then he said, **"That's it! That's it!"**
And he put a sign on the red pony.

The sign said:

THIS PONY DOES NOT WORK!

Then he went back into his shop.

18

A boy came up to the pony
and put in a dime.
But the pony didn't go up and down.

It didn't move.

"I don't know what Rico did,"
the boy said.
"But we can't ride it."

So the children went home.
They were all very sad.

It was very, very quiet
in the flower shop.
And Rico was happy.

But then a little girl came to the shop.
She went up to the little pony
and looked at the sign.
Then she went in to see Rico.

"Can't I ride the pony?" she asked.

"The pony does not work," he told her.

The little girl looked at Rico and said,
"But it is my birthday.
I have just one dime.
All I want for my birthday
is a ride on the pony."

"The pony does not work,"
Rico said again.

"But it is my birthday,"
said the little girl.

Rico looked at the little girl.
She looked very sad.

"One ride," he told her.
"Just one ride, and then go home."

The little girl ran out to the pony.
Rico went with her.

He went to work on the little pony.

Then he said, "You can put your dime in."

The little girl put her dime in.
But the red pony didn't move.

"Wait," Rico told her.
"I will sit on it
and see what I can do."

The little girl looked up
at Rico and laughed.
"Look at you," she said.
"You look funny up there."

Part Three
Rico Pretends

Just then the little red pony
went up and down.
It went up and down, and up and down.

"Stop it! Stop It!" called Rico.

But the pony didn't stop.
Up and down went the little pony,
and up and down went Rico.

The little girl watched and laughed.
"Pretend," she called.
"Pretend you can go very fast."

But Rico didn't want to go very fast.
He just wanted to be quiet.
He wanted to be in the country.
"I'll pretend that I am in the country,"
he thought.
And that's what Rico did.

"The trees are blooming,"
he thought.
"The flowers are blooming, too.
I am all alone,
and it is very quiet."

Now Rico was very, very happy.

But then the little pony came to a stop.
It didn't move.

Then Rico saw the cars.
He saw a big bus.
And he saw his shop.
The trees and the flowers in the country were gone.
He was back in the city.

Rico looked down at the little girl.
"You were right," he said.
"You were very right.
Now I know that it is good to pretend."

Then Rico gave the little girl a dime and went in to look at his flowers.

The little girl put in the dime.
Then she went up and down
on the pony.

"Look at me, look at me!" she called
to Rico.

"Look how fast I can go!"

Rico watched her.
"Yes," he thought.
"The children are right.
It **is** good to pretend."

The little girl went to tell
her friends.
The boys and girls came back
to the flower shop.
And there was a sign on the pony.

The sign said:

This Pony works now.
But you don't have to put in a dime.

RED

Red is sunset
Blazy and bright.
Red is feeling brave
With all your might.

Fire-cracker, fire-engine
Fire-flicker red—
And when you're angry
Red runs through your head.

Red is a show-off
No doubt about it—
But can you imagine
Living without it?

— Mary O'Neill

31

Words That Go Together

Think about how the things go together.

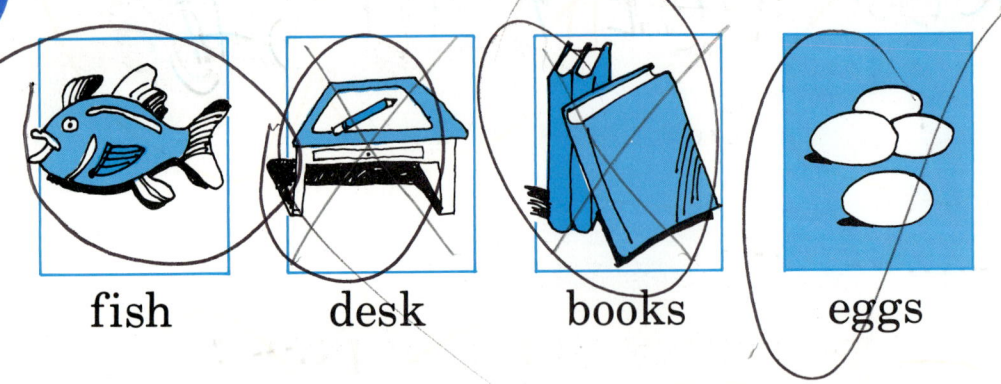

| fish | desk | books | eggs |

Read the words in each box.
The words in each box go together.

Things we work with in school	**Things we eat**
desk books	fish eggs

Desks and books are **things we work with in school.**

Fish and eggs are **things we eat.**

32

2. Write the **things we find in the water.**
Write the **things we ride in.**

| car | fish | bus | frog |

3. Write the **things that fly.**
Write the **things made of paper.**

| bird | book | bee | newspaper |

4. Write the **things you write with.**
Write the **things that a car has.**

| wheel | pencil | seat | crayon |

33

LITTLE BLUE AND LITTLE YELLOW

Leo Lionni

This is Little Blue.
Little Blue lives at home
with his mother and father.
Little Blue has many friends.
But he has one very good friend—
Little Yellow.

Little Yellow lives
with his mother and father, too.
Little Blue and Little Yellow
play together every day.

35

They love to run and jump.
And they love to hide
and find each other.
In school they sit together
all the time.

One day Mother Blue went
to see a friend.
"Now, don't go out!"
she said to Little Blue.

But Little Blue went out.
He went out to look for Little Yellow.
He looked here and there and everywhere
until he found Little Yellow in the park.
Little Blue was very happy
to see his friend.

And Little Yellow was happy, too.
They hugged each other
and hugged each other
until they were green.
Then they went to play in the park.
They ran up and down a big hill.
They ran after Little Red,
and then they went to the lake.
When they were tired,
they went home.

But Mother and Father Blue said,
"You are not our Little Blue.
You are green."

And Mother and Father Yellow said,
"You are not our Little Yellow.
You are green."

Little Blue and Little Yellow
were very sad.
They cried big blue and yellow tears.
They cried and they cried
until they were all tears.

Then Little Blue looked at Little Yellow.
And he saw that Little Yellow
was himself again.
He was not green at all.

"Now they will know who we are,"
said Little Blue.

Mother and Father Blue
were very happy to see Little Blue.
They hugged him and hugged him.
And they hugged Little Yellow, too.

But **look**—
They **all** became green!

"**Now** I know why you were green,"
said Mother Blue.

And they went to Little Yellow's house
to tell Mother and Father Yellow.
They were all so happy
that they laughed and laughed.

Then Little Yellow and Little Blue
ran back to the park to play.

BLUE

Blue is the quiet sea
And the eyes of some people,
And many agree
As they grow older and older
Blue is the scarf
Spring wears on her shoulder.
Blue is twilight,
Shadows on snow,
Blue is feeling
Way down low.

— Mary O'Neill

45

Think of the Sound

Say the word.
Look at the letters in the box.
What sound do you hear?
Find the word in each sentence that has the same sound.
Write the word on your paper.

tr**ai**n

1. I am happy to see my mother paint.
   1. paint
2. It rains every time I see Myra.
3. We can wait for our mother at home.
4. I like to walk on the trail.
5. I put the nail in the doghouse.
6. Can the dog see its tail?
7. Hal wanted to paint his bike red.

Say the word.
Look at the letters in the box.
What sound do you hear?
Find the word in each sentence that has the same sound.
Write the word on your paper.

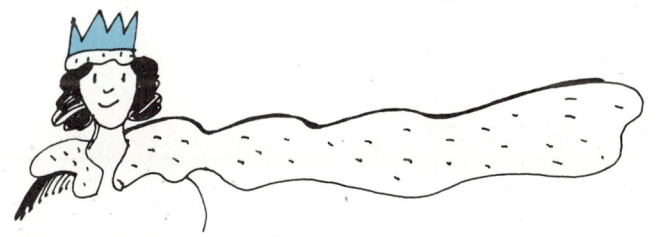

queen

1. We cried when they cut down the tree.
2. I yelled at Bob when I saw him peek.
3. Do you feel like going to the park?
4. Will you meet her by the bus stop?
5. Three frogs sat on the big rock.
6. Bob paints his house green and blue.
7. Linda wants to feed flowers to her bird.

A BABY FOR NICKY

Barbara Brenner

Part One
The Baby in the House

At one time there were three of them—
Father, Mother, and Nicky.
And then the baby came.

"What do you think of her?"
Mother and Father asked Nicky.

"I don't like her," he told them.

Friends came to the house every day.
They came to see the baby.
Nicky didn't like the way
they looked at her.

"Look how **little** she is," they said.

"Look how **quiet** she is," they said.

"Look how **good** she is," they said.

Then they asked Nicky
how he liked the baby.
"I like turtles," he told them.
"I don't like this baby.
You can play with turtles.
But this baby can't do **anything**!"

49

But the baby did not go away.
"Isn't she going to do **anything?**"
Nicky asked Mother.
"Isn't she going to play baseball?
Isn't she going to read a book?
Isn't she going to ride a bike?"

Nicky was disgusted.

One morning Mother told Nicky
to look at the baby.
"See," she said,
"the baby can do things now.
She can eat all alone."

Nicky looked, and there was the baby.
She could eat all alone.
And she could do other things, too.
She could say "boo, boo, boo,"
and pretend her ice cream was a hat.

Mother thought it was funny.
But Nicky didn't.

"Boy," he said.
"I can just **see** you if I did that!"

He was disgusted.
The baby could do anything.
She could sit on the dog.
And she could have piggyback rides.

"How come?" Nicky asked Father.
"How come she can have piggyback rides and I can't?"

"A big boy like you?" said Father.
"You don't want piggyback rides.
But I'll tell you what I'll do.
I'll play baseball with you."

Nicky didn't want to play baseball.
Nicky just wanted a piggyback ride.
Nicky was disgusted.
He was very, very disgusted.

Part Two
A Sister for Nicky

"I know what I'll do," Nicky said to himself one day.
"I'll run away."

Nicky packed his baseball.
He packed his turtle.
He packed his money.
Then he put on his hat.

"Good-by," he called.
"Good-by, I think I'll go now."

Nicky went out the back way.
"Good-by," he called again.

But wait! Someone was there!
"That's just the old baby,"
thought Nicky.
But, no! It was not just the baby.
Butch was there, too.
That no-good, mean Butch.
What did **he** want?

Nicky just had to see.
He walked up to Butch.

"What do **you** want here?" said Nicky.

"Who wants to know?" asked Butch.

"I do," said Nicky.
"And look out for my sister!"

Butch looked at the baby.
"So that's your sister?"
he said in a mean way.

"What do you mean by **that**?" asked Nicky.

"I mean," said Butch, "what good is she?
Can she play baseball?
Can she read a book?
Can she ride a bike?"

"She can't do **anything**!"
And then he laughed.

The baby cried.
She cried and cried and cried.

Nicky looked at Butch.
"You can't do that," he said.
"You can't say things like that
to my sister!"

Butch was sorry.
Nicky made him say
that he was sorry.

"It will be all right now,"
he told the baby.
"That mean old Butch said he was sorry.
Come on, I'll take you in to see Mother."

"What is it?" asked Mother
as they came in.

Nicky said, "Butch!"

"I see," said Mother.

Nicky gave her the baby
and went up to put
his things away.
He put his hat on the bed.
He put away his baseball
and his money.

He put his turtle back in the box.
"I don't think I'll go," he told Mother.

She was very happy.

"I **can't** go," Nicky said.
"I have to take care of her."

"That's right," said Mother.

"She can't do without me," said Nicky.

"That's right," said Mother.

"I'll have to be her friend,"
said Nicky.
"I'll have to help her play baseball
and read books and ride her bike."

Just then the baby said something.
"Nick—y," said the baby.

"How do you like that?" said Nicky.
"She said something.
She said **Nicky!**"

At one time there were three of them—
Father, Mother, and Nicky.
And then the baby came.

Nicky had a sister.

BROTHER

I had a little brother
And I brought him to my mother
And I said I want another
Little brother for a change.
But she said don't be a bother
So I took him to my father
And I said this little bother
Of a brother's very strange.

I asked him why the aves
come down in the fal

My father looked up he big tree.
"The tree takes wate of the ground,"
he said.
"The water goes up
to the green leaves.
The green leaves   r
to make food.
And that is how

"But why do the leaves come down in the fall?" I asked again.

"In the fall," he told me,
"the leaves are old.
They are not green.
They are yellow and red.
They are too old to make food.
So the leaves come off the tree
and fall to the ground."

"Then what does the tree use for food in the winter?" I asked.

"The leaves made food
when they were green," he said.
"They made food for the tree
to use in winter.
When the old leaves fall,
the tree can use the food
that the green leaves made."

My father looked up
at our big tree again.
"It will not be long until
the leaves fall to the ground," he said.
"It will not be long until winter."

**Part Two
The Last Leaves**

My father likes to rake leaves.
But I don't.
I don't like to rake at all.
My father wanted me to rake the leaves
when they came off our big tree.

"Can I wait until all the leaves
are down?" I asked him.

"All right," he said.
"But the day that the last leaves fall,
you will have to rake."

The days were very cold.
And slowly the leaves came down.

One day I went out and looked up
at our big tree.
"They have all come down," I thought.
"And now I will have to rake."

But then I saw two little yellow leaves
way up on the tree.

They looked very old.
I called up to the leaves.
"I don't want to rake, so don't fall.
Use the food you made when you were green.
Then you will not have to fall down."

The days were very, very cold.
But the little yellow leaves didn't fall.
The ground was very, very cold.
But the little yellow leaves didn't fall.

And then, one day, it snowed.

It snowed and snowed and snowed.
I put on my coat and hat and went out.
It was very quiet and very cold.
I could not see the ground.
I could not see the leaves on the ground.

Then I looked up at our big tree.
And there were the little yellow leaves.

"It snowed," I called.
"So I don't have to rake.
You can fall now."

And then, very slowly,
the last leaves of fall came down.

YELLOW

Yellow is the color of the sun
The feeling of fun,
And I guess,
Yellow's the color of
Happiness.

— Mary O'Neill

THE CAT CAME BACK

TEACHER
There was an old yellow cat
Had problems all her own.
Her owners didn't want her,
But she wouldn't leave her home.
They tried everything they could
To keep that cat away,
Even sent her to Australia,
And they told her there to stay.

HONK!

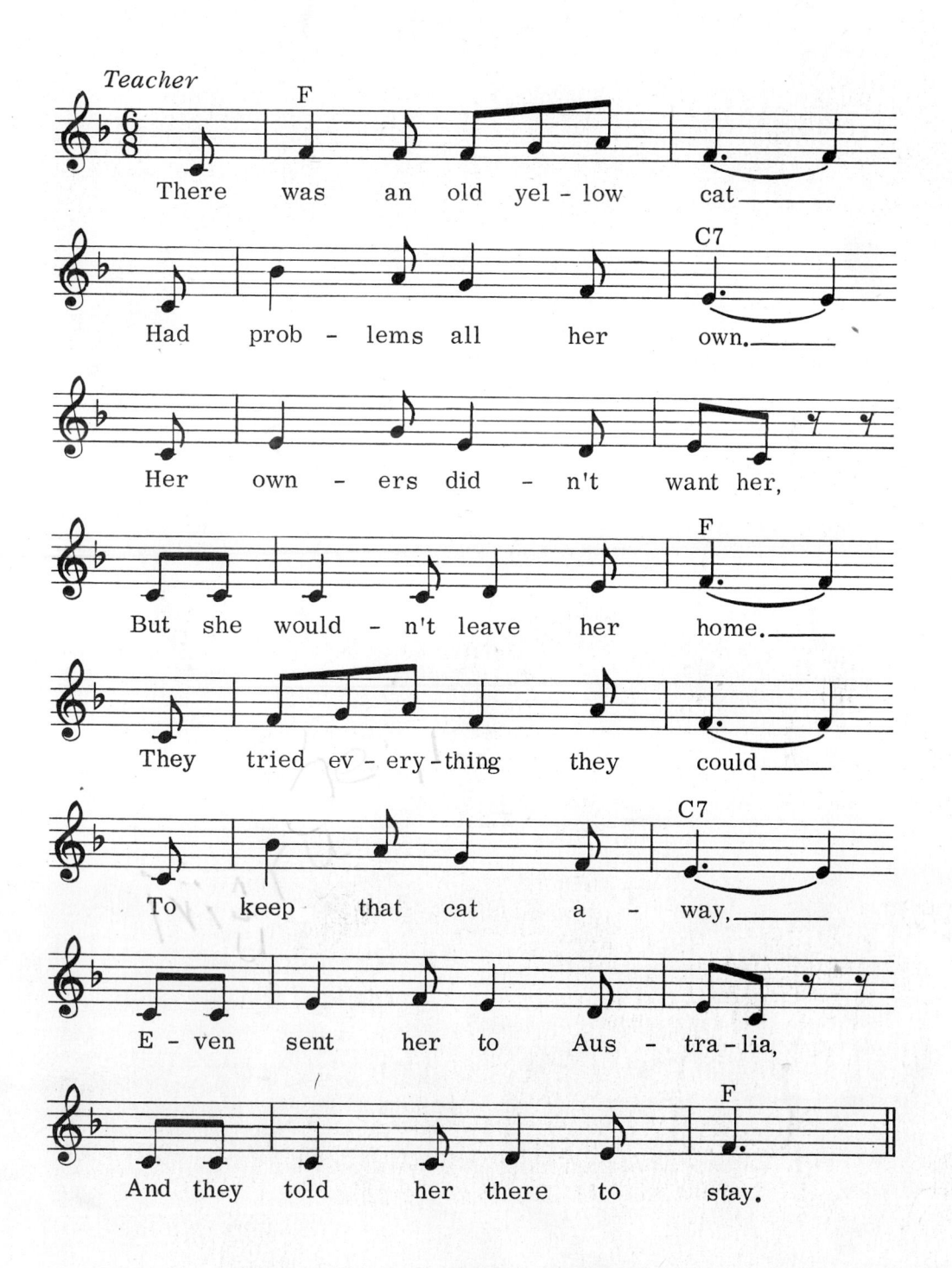

Teacher

There was an old yellow cat
Had problems all her own.
Her owners didn't want her,
But she wouldn't leave her home.
They tried everything they could
To keep that cat away,
Even sent her to Australia,
And they told her there to stay.

CHILDREN
but

The cat came back.
She just couldn't stay too long.
The cat came back.
She just wouldn't stay away.
The cat came back.
They all thought that she was gone.
But the cat came back
On the very next day.

Children

But the cat came back.
She just could-n't stay too long.
The cat came back.
She just would-n't stay a-way.
The cat came back.
They all thought that she was gone.
But the cat came back
On the ver-y next day.

TEACHER

They gave the cat away to
A man with a balloon.
He promised that he'd take her
Right straight up to the moon.
His big balloon came down
About fifty miles away.
Where that man is living now,
No one really dares to say.

CHILDREN

but

The cat came back.

She just couldn't stay too long.

The cat came back.

She just wouldn't stay away.

The cat came back.

They all thought that she was gone.

But the cat came back

On the very next day.

TEACHER
> They gave the yellow cat to
> A boy who had a boat.
> He sailed out on a lake
> With the cat wrapped in his coat.
> He left her on an island
> And thought for sure she'd stay.
> Then he turned his boat around,
> And he sailed home straight away.

CHILDREN

but

The cat came back.

She just couldn't stay too long.

The cat came back.

She just wouldn't stay away.

The cat came back.

They all thought that she was gone.

But the cat came back

On the very next day.

TEACHER
> At last they took that cat and,
> They thought it would be best
> To put her on a train
> That was going way out west.
> The train was speeding down the track
> When it struck a rock.
> And all the people on that train
> Suffered greatly from the shock.

CHILDREN

but

The cat came back.
She just couldn't stay too long.
The cat came back.
She just wouldn't stay away.
The cat came back.
They all thought that she was gone.
But the cat came back
On the very next day.

TEACHER
>They never did stop trying
>To drive that cat away.
>They had a different idea
>Every other day.
>They even mailed her in a box
>The world all around,
>But every time she'd come right back
>To her very own home ground.

CHILDREN

yes

The cat came back.

She just couldn't stay too long.

The cat came back.

She just wouldn't stay away.

The cat came back.

They all thought that she was gone.

But the cat came back

On the very next day.

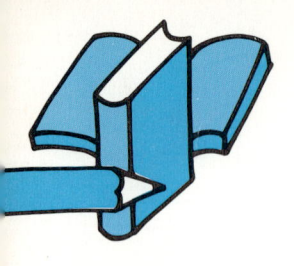

Words Work Together

Sometimes two words can be put together to make one new word.

flower + pot => flowerpot

Put the words below together to make a new word.
Write the new word on your paper.

shoe + maker   1. <u>shoemaker</u>
birth + day   2. _____
base + ball   3. _____
lunch + room   4. _____
after + noon   5. _____
rain + coat   6. _____
dog + house   7. _____
hat + box   8. _____

Find the word in the box that goes with each picture.
Then put the two picture words together to make one new word.
Write the new word on your paper.

| house | tree | book | bird |
| ball | foot | boat | cook |

1. football
2. _____
3. _____
4. _____
5. _____

87

A Present for the Queen

Part One
What Will I Give the Queen?

At one time there was a king
who was very happy.
He had houses and ponies
and all the money he wanted.
But there was one thing the king
did not have.
He did not have a birthday present
for the queen.

For the queen had houses and ponies
and all the money she wanted.
So the king did not know
what to give her for a present.

"How can I surprise my queen?"
the king asked himself.
"What will be a very good present?"

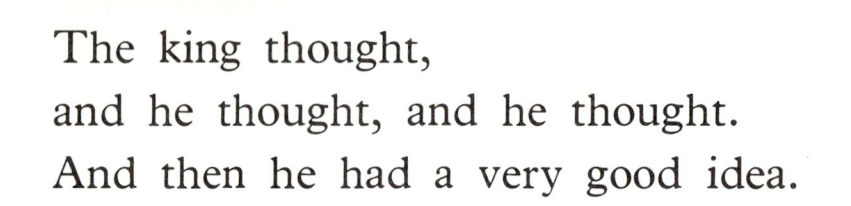

The king thought,
and he thought, and he thought.
And then he had a very good idea.

"**I will give my queen a bed!**" he said.

The queen did not have a bed.
No one had a bed.
For, at that time, no one had **thought** of a bed.

The king called his little helper and said,
"I want you to make a bed."

"How big is a bed?"
asked the little helper.

The little helper had no idea.
At that time, no one had seen a bed.

"How big **is** a bed?"
the king asked himself.
The king thought,
and he thought, and he thought.
And then he had a very good idea.

The bed must be
just right for the queen.

**Part Two
How BIG Is a Bed?**

The king called the queen and said,
"Lie down, my queen.
Lie down so I can see
how big you are."

Then, with his big feet, he counted
**six feet long
and
three
feet
wide.**

The king called his little helper. "Make the bed six feet long and three feet wide," he said. "That will be just right for the queen."

So, with his little feet,
the little helper
counted

                        **six feet long
                            and
                           three
                            feet
                           wide**.

And then he made a bed for the queen.

When the bed was made,
the little helper went to the king.
The king was very happy to see the bed.
He called the queen in, and said,
"Lie down on the bed, my queen."

**But
the bed was too little for the queen!**

The king was not at all happy.
"Why is this bed too little?"
he asked the little helper.
"I told you to make it
just right for the queen."
The little helper was very sad.

Why was the bed too little for the queen?

**Part Three
How BIG Is a Foot?**

The little helper thought,
and he thought, and he thought.

And then he had a very good idea.

"My bed was six **helper's** feet long and three **helper's** feet wide," he said to himself.

"And that is not as big as a bed that is six **king's** feet long and three **king's** feet wide.

"I can make the king a bed that is just right for the queen,"

But I have to know how big his foot is!"

...le helper thought
...thought, and he thought.
...en he had a very good idea.

"I can make a copy of the king's foot," he said to himself.
"And then I will know how big his foot is."

So the little helper
went to see the king.
And the king let the little helper
make a copy of his foot.

With the copy of the king's foot,
the little helper counted

                        six feet long
                              and
                             three
                              feet
                              wide.

And then he made a bed for the queen.

On her birthday the king called the queen in and told her to lie down. And, this time,
the bed was just right for the queen!

The queen was very, very happy
with her present.
"I love my surprise,"
she told the king.

And the king was happy, too.
He called the little helper,
and they had a big party.

And now, when the queen says,
"My bed is

>
> six feet long
> and
> three
> feet
> wide,"

we all know that it is

**six king's feet long
and
three
king's
feet
wide.**

And we all know **just** how big that is!

The Princess and the Pea

The Players:

King

Queen

Prince   Helper

Princess

Time: Afternoon
Place: A castle

Act One
How Can You Tell?

         *(King, Queen, and Prince
         are in the castle.
         They look very sad.)*
King: *(looks at Prince)*
         You must find a wife soon.
         And your wife must be a princess.
         Don't you know a princess
         who could be your wife?
Prince: Yes, I know a princess.
         But I don't know if she is
         a *real* princess or not.
         My wife must be a *real* princess.
Queen: How can you tell
         if she is a *real* princess?

Prince: I don't know how to tell.
But I will think of a way.
Helper: *(walks in and goes to Queen)*
There is a woman at the castle door.
She says she is lost.
She wants to stay here
until morning.
Queen: She may come in.
Take her to the kitchen.
Give her something to eat.
Helper: I am sorry.
I can't do that.
She won't go into the kitchen.

King: (looks at Helper)
Why won't she go into the kitchen?

Helper: She says she is a princess.
A princess can't go into the kitchen.

Prince: (runs to Helper)
Is she a *real* princess?

Helper: I don't know.
How can you tell
if she is a *real* princess?

Prince: I don't know.
But I will think of a way.
I *must* think of a way.
(They are all quiet.
Prince walks up and down.)

Prince: That's it!
I have a good thought.

Queen: What is your thought?
Prince: The princess can stay here.
We will give her a soft bed.
But I will find a little green pea.
I will put it
under the mattresses of the bed.
King: I think that's a silly thing to do.
Why will you do that?

Prince: The princess will lie down on the bed. The little green pea will be under the mattresses of the bed. A *real* princess will feel the little green pea. We can tell if she is a *real* princess!

Queen: *(to Prince)* That's a very good thought. Put a little green pea under the mattresses. We will see if she can feel it. *(to Helper)* Go give the princess something to eat.

Prince: I will look for soft mattresses.

Queen: I will look for soft mattresses, too.

King: I think this is a silly idea. But I will look for a little green pea.

Prince: Soon we will know if she is a *real* princess.
(They all go out.)

Act Two
A *Real* Princess

*(Prince comes in.
He has three mattresses.)*

Prince: The mattresses will make a soft bed. But I must have more mattresses.

Queen: *(comes in)* Here are more mattresses.

King: *(comes in)* Here is a little green pea.

Prince: First, I'll put the little green pea on the bed.
Then I'll put the mattresses on the little green pea.

King: I think this is a *very* silly idea!

Queen: *(gives two mattresses to Prince)* Here are two blue mattresses.

King: *(gives two mattresses to Prince)* Here are two red mattresses.

Queen: *(gives two mattresses to Prince)* Here are two green mattresses.

Prince: Thank you for your help. This is a very soft bed for the princess.

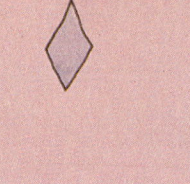

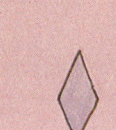

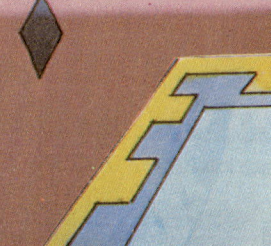

113

Queen: The little green pea
is under the mattresses.
We will see if the princess
can feel it.
We will know if she
is a *real* princess.

Prince: Yes, soon we will know.
I might like the princess very much.
She might like me, too.
She might be a *real* princess.
The princess might marry me.
She might be my wife.

King: Yes, she might do that.
But I think this is a *very* silly idea!
(Princess and Helper come in.)

Helper: Here is the princess.
She has had something to eat.

King: Was the food good?

Princess: It was very good, thank you.

Queen: Here is a bed for you.
It is a very soft bed.

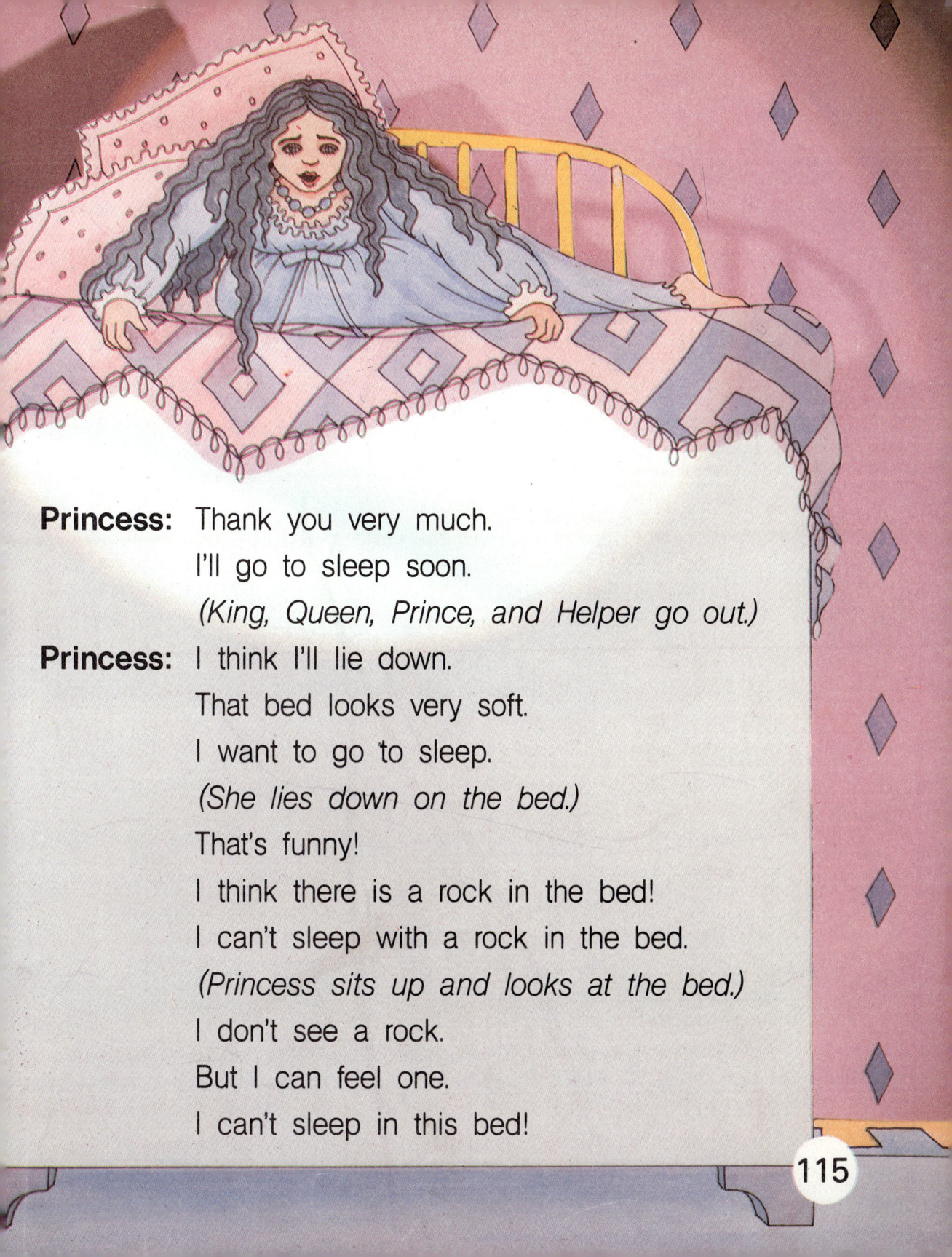

Princess: Thank you very much.
I'll go to sleep soon.
(King, Queen, Prince, and Helper go out.)
Princess: I think I'll lie down.
That bed looks very soft.
I want to go to sleep.
(She lies down on the bed.)
That's funny!
I think there is a rock in the bed!
I can't sleep with a rock in the bed.
(Princess sits up and looks at the bed.)
I don't see a rock.
But I can feel one.
I can't sleep in this bed!

Prince: *(comes in)*
Why can't you sleep in it?
Princess: There is a rock in the bed!
Prince: Now I know that you are a *real* princess!
Princess: How do you know that?
Prince: There is a little green pea under the mattresses.
Only a *real* princess could feel the little green pea.
Princess: I thought it was a big rock!
Prince: I like you.
Will you marry me?
Will you be my wife?

Princess: Yes, I'll marry you.
I like you, too.

Prince: Now I am very happy.
(King, Queen, and Helper come in.)

King: I am happy, too.
But I think it was
a very, very silly idea!

Princess: I think so, too.

Prince: I don't think it was silly.
Now we know you are a *real* princess.
You are the only *real* princess
that I know.
And you are going to be my wife!

What Is the Big Idea?

Each sentence below says something about flowers.

> Flowers are many colors.
> The flowers next to the school are yellow.
> The flowers at John's house are red.
> My grandma gave me blue flowers.
> My friend Nicky had gold flowers.

1. What sentence tells what the other sentences are about? Write the sentence on your paper.

> Flowers are many colors.
> My grandma gave me blue flowers.

1. Flowers are many colors.

Each sentence tells about the park.

    Susy goes to the park to play ball.
    John rides his bike in the park.
    Fred sits in the park and reads.
    Many children are in the park.

2. What sentence tells about the others?

    Fred sits in the park and reads.
    Many children are in the park.

Each sentence tells about Sam's books.

    Sam reads many books.
    He reads books about cars.
    He reads books about the country.
    In school, he read a book about a dog.

3. What sentence tells about the others?

    Sam reads many books.
    He reads books about the country.

COLORS

Everywhere you look there are colors.
Sometimes colors tell how things look.
Sometimes colors go with how you feel.
Other words can tell how you feel, too.

Thinking About "Colors"

1. What color words did you read about in "Colors?"
2. What words tell you how Rico feels when he sits on the red pony?
3. Can you find words that tell you how Nicky feels when he sees Butch?
4. If you say, "I feel blue," what do you mean?

BEING ME

There are all kinds of people.
But there is no one just like you.
There are things that you can do.
There are other things you can't do.
In "Being Me," you will read about a boy
who finds out that he is a very
good friend for someone.

You will read about a girl who finds out
that she likes the way she is.
As you read, look for other people
who find out what they can do.

Okay everybody, listen to this:
I am tired of being smaller
Than you
And them
And him
And trees and buildings.
So watch out
All you gorillas and adults
Beginning tomorrow morning
Boy
Am I going to be taller.

—Karla Kuskin

123

NEVER GREAT

Elizabeth Levy

Part One
Not Bad

When Larry did things, people said,
"That's good."
Or people said, "Not bad."
But people never said
what Larry did was great.
And Larry wanted to do something great.

One time Larry was at home
with his father.
His father asked,
"Would you like to help cook the eggs
for lunch?"

"Yes, I would," said Larry.

So Larry helped cook the eggs.
But they did not come out just right.
The yellow was all funny.

Larry's father saw that Larry
didn't look happy.
"The eggs are not so bad," he said.

"I know," said Larry.
"But they are not so good.
They are not great eggs."

One time at school
Larry had to paint a flower.
Larry painted a blue and yellow one.
He thought it looked good.

Then Larry saw the flower
that one of the other boys had painted.
It was big and red.
It had a bird on it.

"My flower is not bad," thought Larry.
"But that one is great.
Why couldn't I paint a great flower?"

Larry thought he would never do anything great.

Part Two
New Boy in School

One morning a new boy came
to Larry's school.
"This is Ted," said the teacher.
The boys and girls said,
"Good morning."
But Ted did not say a word.
He did not look at the teacher
or the boys and girls.
He just looked down at his shoes.

The teacher told the new boy
to sit by Larry.
"Good morning, Ted," Larry said.
"Do you want to see the flower
I painted?"

Ted was very quiet.
He did not say "yes" or "no."

Larry went with Ted when it was time for lunch.
"Come and sit with me," Larry said.
Ted did not say a word.
But he went and sat with Larry.

On the playground, Larry said to Ted, "Let's play catch."

Ted looked down.
He said, "No."

And that was all he said that day.

Ted was so quiet
that no one thought of him.
No one but Larry.

Every day Larry sat with Ted at lunch.
And sometimes Larry sat with Ted
to help him with his work.
But for a long time,
Ted did not say anything.

Then one day on the playground, Larry saw Ted looking at him.

"Would you like to play catch today?" Larry asked.

"Yes," Ted said.

Ted threw the ball to Larry.
Larry did not catch it.
The ball was on the ground.

Larry threw it back to Ted.

Ted could catch the ball.

"You are good at playing catch,"
Larry said.
"I am not so great at it.
I am not so great at anything."

Ted looked at Larry.

"Yes, you are," he said.

"You are a great friend."

134

This Is My Rock

This is my rock,
And here I run
To steal the secret of the sun.

This is my rock,
And here run I
Before the night has swept the sky.

This is my rock,
This is the place
I meet the evenings face to face.

—David McCord

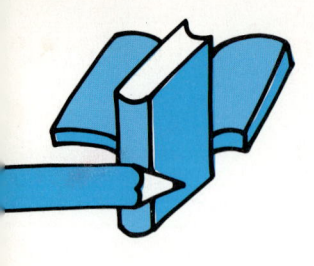

Make Opposites

Look at the word with a line under it in each sentence.

The boy rides <u>up</u>.   The boy rides <u>down</u>.

The words <u>up</u> and <u>down</u> are **opposites**.

Find the word in a box that is the opposite of each word below. Write the two words on your paper.

| sad | down | good | little | go | country |

1. happy   <u>sad</u>
2. stop   _____
3. big   _____
4. up   _____
5. bad   _____
6. city   _____

136

Look at the word with a line under it in each sentence.

Find the word in the box that is the opposite.

Write the sentences on your paper.

| out | found | old | cold | country |

1. The bird is <u>in</u> the cage.
   The bird is <u>out</u> of the cage.

2. The soup is very <u>hot.</u>
   The ice cream is very ___.

3. Kate has a <u>new</u>, red bike.
   Sam has an ___ blue bike.

4. John <u>lost</u> his lizard.
   Ann ___ John's lizard.

5. Linda lives in the <u>city.</u>
   Fred lives in the ___.

The Song of Little Frog
George Richards

**Part One
Frogs Don't Sing**

Little Frog lived by a lake.
He did not have many things.
He had one old book that he read again and again.
He had one old pot to cook in.
And he had a little bed to sleep in.

Little Frog did not have much.
But he was happy.
Little Frog liked to look at the flowers.
He liked to dance.
But more than anything Little Frog
liked to sing.

At that time, other frogs did not sing.
"Frogs just don't sing," they said.
"That's for the birds.
We all know that!"

But Little Frog loved to sing.
He couldn't help it.
He would sing as much as he could.
But he didn't sing when he was around the other frogs.
He would sing just when he was alone.

One day Little Frog wanted to take
a walk in the woods.
On the way to the woods he saw
something that made him stop.
He saw many, many frogs
around a big tree.

"What are you doing?" asked Little Frog.

"Look at that!" said one of the frogs.

Little Frog saw a sign on the tree.
The sign said:

IMPORTANT
ALL FROGS ARE TO
COME TO OLD FROG'S
HOUSE TODAY AT
THREE O'CLOCK

"What is this all about?"
asked Little Frog.

"I don't know," said a frog.
"But the sign says it is important.
So let's go."

"What could be so important?"
thought Little Frog.

**Part Two
At Old Frog's House**

When Little Frog got to Old Frog's house,
many frogs were there.
At last Old Frog put up his hands,
and all the frogs became very quiet.

"I have something important to tell you,"
said Old Frog.
"It is about the big bird."

"Not that again," said some of the frogs.

"Do you call **that** important?"
said some of the other frogs.

You see, Old Frog had said many things about the big bird.
He had said,
"The big bird is very big.
The big bird is very scary.
The big, scary bird could eat the trees.
The big, scary bird could eat the houses, if he wanted to."

Then he had said,
"The big bird could come here one day."

But the frogs would say,
"Look, Old Frog,
we want our trees.
We want our houses.
We do **not** want a big, scary bird
around here.
If we see him coming,
we will tell him to go away from us."

So that's what the frogs said
when they went to Old Frog's house.

"But—" said Old Frog.

"That's right," said one frog.
"We will tell him to go away."

"But—" said Old Frog again.

"We will tell that big bird
that we want him to go away from us,"
said one of the other frogs.

"That is good," said Old Frog.
"I am happy to know that you can take care of things.
You see, the big bird is coming

RIGHT NOW!"

"Right now!" said one frog.

"Coming right now!"
said one of the other frogs.

The frogs ran out of Old Frog's house.
They forgot to take the hats.
They forgot to take the coats.
And they forgot to tell the big bird to go away.

Little Frog was alone with Old Frog.
What would they do?

Part Three
What Little Frog Did

Little Frog looked out.
He looked up and up and up.
He saw the big bird.
And do you know what the
big bird was about to do?
He was about to eat a tree.

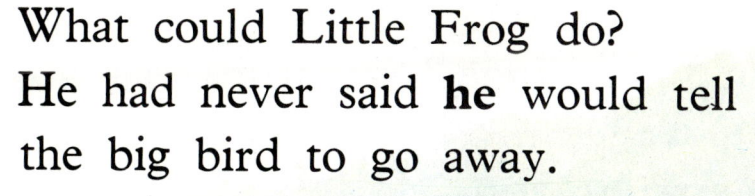

What could Little Frog do?
He had never said **he** would tell
the big bird to go away.

"What can I do?" he said to Old Frog.

"You must do something no other frog can do," said Old Frog.

"I can do only one thing that no other frog can do. I can sing."

"You sing?" said Old Frog.

"Only when I am alone," said Little Frog. "You see the other frogs say that singing is for the—BIRDS!"

Little Frog ran out of the house
and up to the big bird's feet.
Little Frog looked way up at the big bird.

The big bird looked way down at Little Frog.
"What does that little thing want?" he thought.

Just then Little Frog began to sing.

    Nee-dee-bup
    nee-dee-bup
    ribbit, ribbit.
    Nee-dee-bup
    nee-dee-bup
    ribbit, ribbit.

The big bird put down the tree
he was going to eat.
"I didn't know frogs could sing," he thought.

Little Frog sang some more.
The big bird was so happy with the song that he began to dance.
He danced and danced.
His big, scary feet moved up and down.

Little Frog sang some more.
And the big bird danced on and on.

The big bird danced so much
that he began to go up.

He went up   and up   and up
until he could not be seen at all.

Everyone ran out from the houses.

154

"You are **some** little frog," they cried.
"You made the big bird go away."
"You did it!"

Then one frog said,
"If you help us, we might get to sing like you."

"Yes, we might get to sing like you,"
said the other frogs.
"And we would like that very much."

Little Frog still lives by the lake.
But there is a sign next to his house now.
The sign says:

LITTLE FROG
TEACHER OF
SINGING
TO ALL FROGS

Many frogs sing now.
They don't think singing is something
a frog does not do.
And at night, if you are by a lake,
the frogs might sing this song for you.

Nee-dee-bup nee-dee-bup rib-bit, rib-bit.

Nee-dee-bup nee-dee-bup rib-bit, rib-bit.

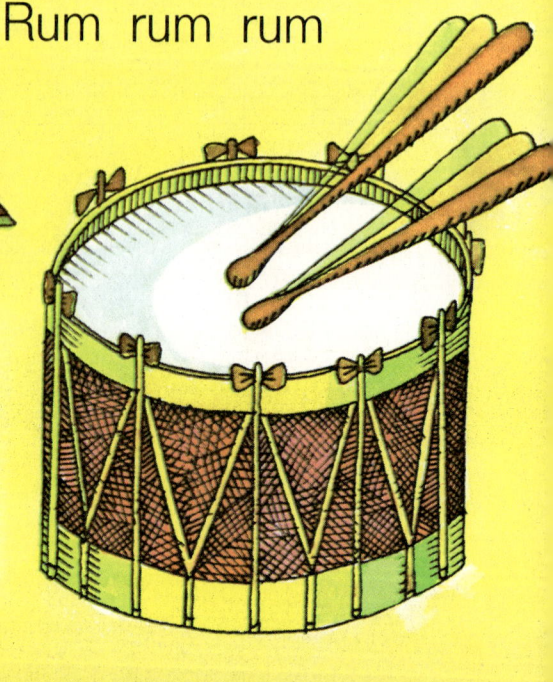

Sing Along

Clock's Song

Tick tock tick
Tick tock tick
Ticka tocka
Ticka tocka
Click click click
DING!

Drum's Song

Ta tum
Ta tum
Ta tum tum tum
Ta rum
Ta rum
Ta rum rum rum
Rumbly dum
Bumbly rum
Rum rum rum

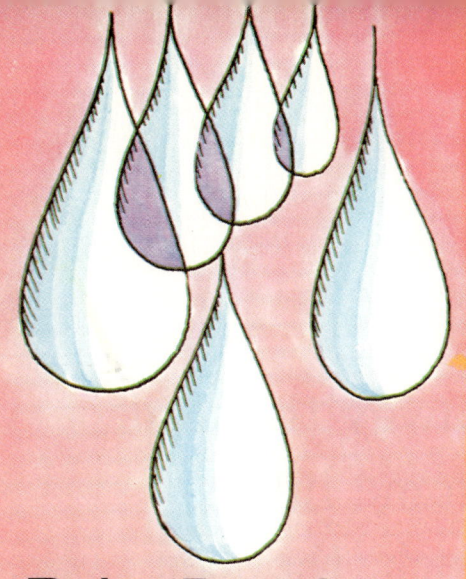

Rain Drop's Song

Tinca tinca tinc
Plip plip plip
Plink plink plink
Drip drip drip
Plippety ploppety plop
Drippety drippety drop!
Drop
    Drop
        Drop.

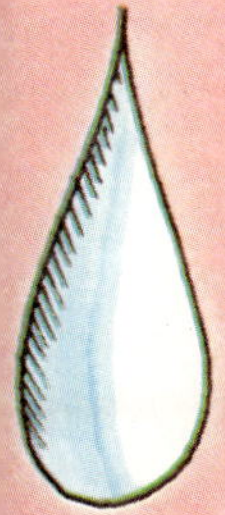

Bee's Song

Buzz buzz
Bee bop
Buzz
Bee bop
Bee bop
Buzz
  zzzz
    zzzz

Singing isn't just for the birds!

Why?

Read the sentences.

> Kate forgot to put away the food.
> Kate's cat wanted some lunch.
> When Kate came back, the food was gone.

1. Write the sentence that tells why the food was gone.

   > Kate put the food away.
   > Kate's cat had the food for lunch.

   1. Kate's cat had the food for lunch.

Read the sentences.

> Larry wanted to paint his bike red.
> A friend gave him some red paint.
> Now, Larry's coat has red paint on it.

2. Write the sentence that tells why Larry's coat has paint on it.

> Larry got paint on his coat when he painted his bike.
> Larry did not have his coat on.

Read the sentences.
> The king's donkey wanted to eat some flowers.
> The donkey saw many flowers on the hill.
> The king couldn't find his donkey.

3. Write the sentence that tells why the king couldn't find his donkey.

> The king's donkey went to sleep.
> The king's donkey went to eat the flowers on the hill.

UNCLE HARRY

Gerlinde Schneider

Part One
No Room for a Kitten

One day Uncle Harry went out
for a walk.
He saw a little kitten
in the big old tree in the park.
The kitten looked very, very sad.
Uncle Harry didn't like kittens.
But he didn't like to see one
looking so sad.

So Uncle Harry got the kitten out of the tree.
He put her on the ground.
"Go away," he said.
"Go on—walk!"

And that is just what the kitten did.
She walked.
She walked right in back of Uncle Harry.
Uncle Harry didn't see the kitten
until he got home.
Then he said,
"Off with you—go away!"
And he went into the house.

The next morning,
when Uncle Harry came out,
the kitten was still there.

Uncle Harry got some milk
from the house.
"Why did I get you out of that tree?"
he said.
"Now, have this milk.
Then I will take you
to the Lost-and-Found."

The kitten had the milk.
Uncle Harry got a box
and put the kitten in it.

At the Lost-and-Found
a man looked in the box.
"We can't take her," he said.
"We don't take kittens here.
You want the Pound."

At the Pound a woman looked in the box.
"Sorry," she said.
"We don't have room for one more animal in this Pound."

So Uncle Harry went out.

Then he saw a boy.
He asked him if he would like a kitten.
But the boy said he had a dog
that didn't like kittens.

Then a girl walked by.
Uncle Harry asked her
if she wanted a kitten.
The girl looked in the box.
The girl said she had a kitten
just like the one Uncle Harry had.

"Her name is Minx," she said.

"Minx," Uncle Harry said.
"That's a very good name.
Yes, Minx is a good name."

So Uncle Harry went home.
He put the box down.
The kitten jumped out of the box
and up on Uncle Harry.

"You stop that right now,"
said Uncle Harry.

But the kitten just sat very still.

Part Two
A Home for Minx

The next day, Uncle Harry had an idea. This time he put the kitten in a basket and went to the bakery.

"Do you need a cat?" he asked the man in the bakery.
"She could catch mice for you."

"There are no mice in my bakery," the man said.

"No mice," said Uncle Harry.
By this time he was not very happy.

He walked to the next street.
He put the kitten down on the ground.
"Stay here," he said.
"Someone will find you."

Then Uncle Harry began to walk home.
But the kitten jumped up
and ran up the street after him.

And so they went home together.

Some days after that, Uncle Harry took the kitten back to the Pound. He took her in a basket.

"Good to see you," said the woman at the Pound.
"We just gave away a dog. Now we have room for your kitten."

Uncle Harry took the kitten out of the basket.

But he did not put her down.
He looked at her for a long time.

Then he said, "I will call you Minx.
You will come home with me."

Now, when Uncle Harry walks up
the street, Minx walks with him.

Use a Map

Look at the words in the boxes.
Find a word for each sentence that tells Hal how to get to Liza's house.
Use the map to help you.
Write the sentences on your paper.

| blue | school | woods | playground |

1. First, walk by the <u>woods</u>.
2. Next, walk by the ____.
3. Last, walk by the ____.
4. Liza's house is painted ____.

Look at the words in the boxes.
Find a word for each sentence that tells
Little Bear how to find Mother Bear.
Use the map to help you.
Write the sentences on your paper.

| woods | rock | hill | water |

1. First, run up the ____.
2. Next, walk by the ____.
3. Last, go around the ____.
4. Mother Bear is next to the big ____.

LITTLE LEROY

George McCue

Part One
Time to Eat

Leroy was a little blue fish.
His home was next to a rock.
Leroy was very little.
But some of his friends were very big.
Leroy's big friends lived a long way from his rock.
But he saw them every day.
Every day they would swim by to see Leroy.

"Time to eat," Leroy would say when they came.

The big fish had tiny animals on them.
They did not like the tiny animals.
But Leroy did.

Leroy ate the tiny animals
off the big fish.
The big fish got cleaned up.
And Leroy got his lunch.

Henry was one of the fish that
Leroy cleaned.
Henry was very big, as big as a man.
Leroy liked to see Henry every day.
Henry gave Leroy a big lunch.

One day Henry was very tired.
He had played too much
with the other big fish.
"I don't think I'll swim over
to Leroy's rock today," he thought.

The next day Henry was still tired.
He still did not want
to swim over to see Leroy.

Two of the other big fish came by
to see Henry.

"Swim over and see Leroy," they said.
"He wants more to eat."

But Henry said,
"I am too tired.
If Leroy wants more to eat,
he will have to come and see me."

For three days, Henry did not swim over
to see Leroy.
By that time, Henry had
many little animals on him.
"I think I will go and see Leroy today,"
Henry thought.
"He will be happy to see me."

So Henry went to Leroy's rock.
He wanted to get cleaned up.
But Henry was in for a big surprise.
Leroy was not there.

Part Two
Where is Leroy?

"Where is that Leroy?" Henry yelled as another big fish swam by. "I have to get cleaned up."

"Leroy is gone," said the other fish.

"Gone? Why?" cried Henry.

"You would not come to see him," said the other fish. "He had to have some more to eat. So he swam away to look for more."

"Leroy will have to come back,"
thought Henry.
"He needs me to give him lunch,
and I need him to get cleaned up."

Henry waited by Leroy's rock,
but Leroy did not come back.
Henry was not happy at all.
By this time, he had many little animals
on him.
He wanted to get cleaned up.
He waited a long time, but Leroy still
did not come back.
So Henry went to look for Leroy.

He swam and swam all day.
He swam until he was very tired.
Then he saw something
that made him stop.

There, next to a little rock, he saw
a big fish and a little fish.
Henry swam up to them.
And there was Leroy!
Leroy was eating some lunch
off the big fish.

"Leroy, Leroy," Henry called.
"I am so happy to see you.
Why did you go away?"

"Look, Henry," Leroy said.
"I had to have some more to eat.
You would not come to see me.
So I came to see you.
But on my way, I saw another big fish.
He gave me my lunch,
so I stayed with him."

Henry looked sad.
"You are my good friend," Henry said.
"Come back, Leroy,
and I will never leave you alone again."

So Henry and Leroy swam off together.
They swam back to Leroy's rock.
Henry got cleaned up.
And Leroy got his lunch.
Then Henry swam home.

Henry was never too tired
to see Leroy again.
He swam to Leroy's rock every day.
He found out that little friends
were very good to have.

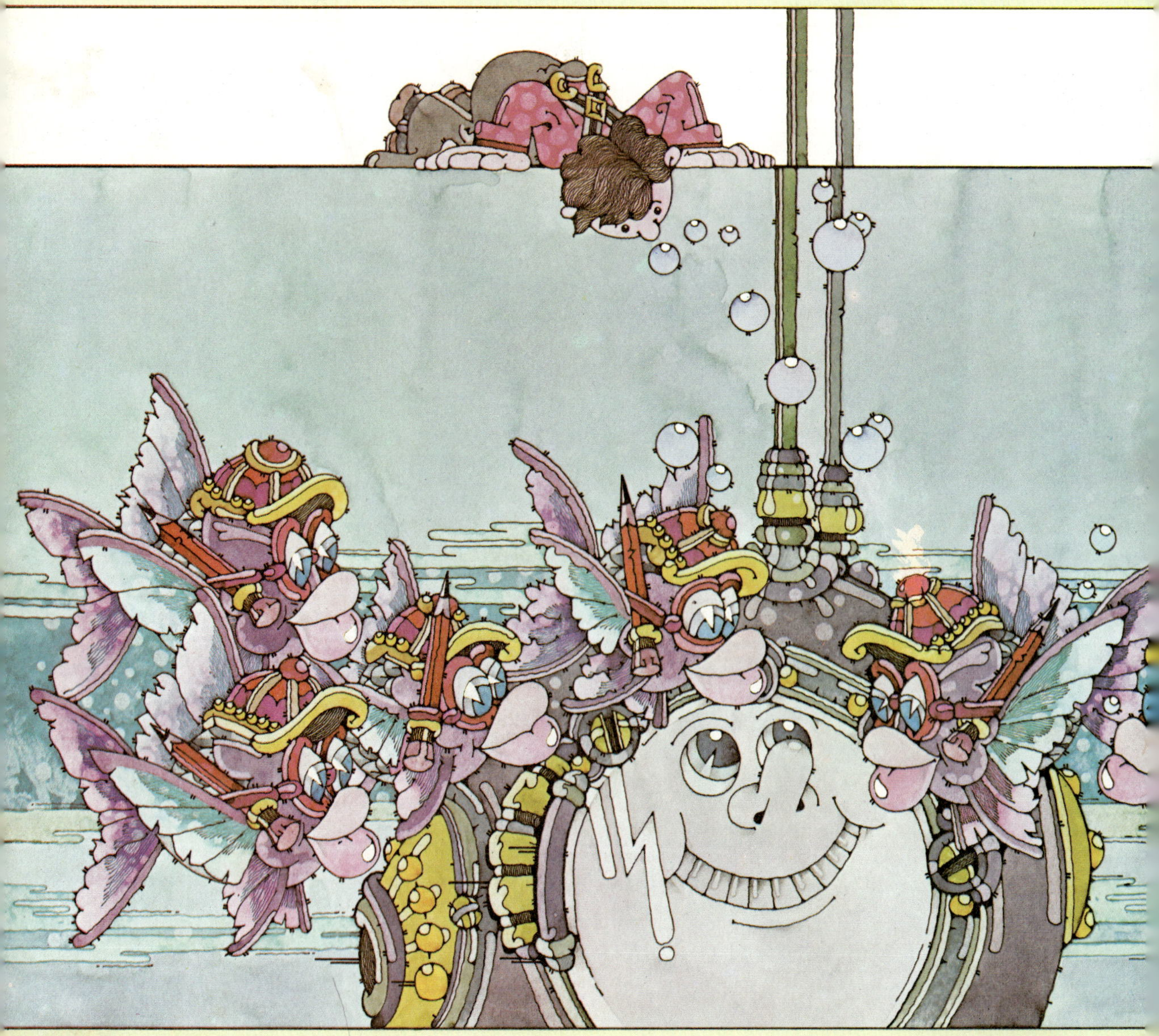

THE SCHOOL OF FISH

I went to find a school of fish
just the other day.
I looked and looked both up and down
and every other way.

But I could not find a schoolroom
with little fish inside.
And I could not find a teacher
who was teaching on the tide.

Then I saw a lot of fish
who all looked just the same.
They swam and swam round and round
as if it were a game.

"A school of fish is what we are,"
they shouted out to me.
"You must have come from very far.
What did you want to see?"

—Alma Whitney

In the Water

Sally R. Bell

There are many animals
that live in the water.
Some of them are fish.
But there are other animals
that live in the water, too.
They are not fish.
Sometimes they don't look
like animals at all.
But they are animals.

A fish is an animal
that lives in the water.
A fish has no hands or feet.
It has fins.

The fins help it move in the water.
A fish has scales on it.
The scales are all over the fish.

This animal is a fish.
It has scales and fins.
It can move in the water.
It is called a **clown fish.**

The clown fish has many colors on it.
That is why it is called a clown fish.
The colors are on the scales.

The clown fish has a friend.
The friend is not a fish.
It looks like a flower.
But it is an animal.

The animal does not have fins.
It does not have scales.
It can't move in the water.

So the clown fish takes food
to its friend.
If the clown fish wants to hide,
it can hide in the animal.

This animal lives in the water.
It has fins, so it can move
in the water.
But it has no scales.

It is called a **sea horse**.
Its head looks like the head
of a horse.

The sea horse has a long tail.
It holds on to things with its tail.

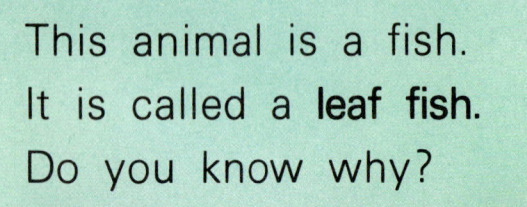

This animal is a fish.
It is called a **leaf fish**.
Do you know why?

The leaf fish has fins and scales.
It can move in the water.
But it likes to stay still.
Other fish see the leaf fish.
They think it is just a leaf.
So the leaf fish can hide
from other fish!

There are many kinds of animals
that live in the water.
There are many kinds of fish.
There are other animals, too.

Some of them are friends,
like the clown fish and its friend.
Some of them like to be alone.
The sea horse and the leaf fish
like to be alone.

You can find out more about
the animals that live in the water.
There are many books about them.

Find the Sounds

Say the words and look at the letters in the box.
What sounds do you hear?
Find the words in each sentence that have the same sounds.
Write the words on your paper.

c[ow]   cl[ou]d

1. We found a little brown mouse.
   1. found, brown, mouse
2. He ran all around until we made him go out of the house.
3. We saw him playing on the ground down by the big tree.
4. Now his friend is a mouse who lives in the tree.

c|oi|n   b|oy|

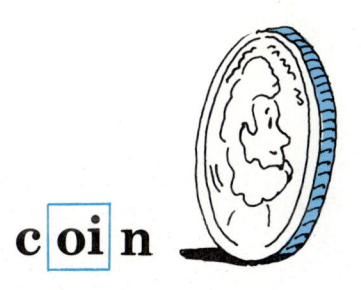

5. Leroy went to join the other boys in the kitchen.
6. They helped their Uncle Roy as he began to boil water.
7. Then they played with a blue toy.

Now find all the words with the four sounds you know in the story below. Write the words on your paper.

c|oi|n   c|ow   b|oy   cl|ou|d

The woman took some soil and put it into a brown flowerpot.
Then she put a red flower in the pot.
She gave it to a boy in the house.

Alma Whitney

**Part One
A Very Good Girl**

My mother said it would be good
for me to know Betsy.
"Betsy is a very good girl,"
my mother said.
"She always makes her bed.
And she always eats her beets.
That's what her mother says."

I didn't always make my bed.
And I never ate beets.

My mother said it would be good
for me to know Betsy.
And then Betsy came to our house.
And we found out she could do **more**
than her mother said.

Betsy came into the house
with her mother.
Her mother saw our piano.
"Play the piano," she said.

So Betsy played the piano.

"Read big words," her mother said.
So Betsy read big words.

And at lunch her mother said,
"Eat your beets."
So Betsy ate her beets.
She ate more beets than my mother did.
She ate more beets than her mother did.

But she kicked me, too.
And no one saw her do that.

I wanted to tell my mother
that Betsy kicked me.
But there was never time to tell her.

My mother said that it would be
so much fun for Betsy to sleep
at our house.

"So much fun," said Betsy's mother.
"So much fun," said Betsy.

I did not get to tell my mother
that Betsy kicked me.

Betsy's mother went home.
And Betsy was in our house.

Part Two
Time for Bed

"I want that bed," Betsy said
when she saw my room.
"That's my bed," I said.

But my mother said it was all right
for Betsy to have my bed.
She said I could sleep in it any time.
My mother said it would be such fun
for me to sleep in the other bed.

So we went to bed.

"Andy, Andy," Betsy called.

"I am Sandy," I said.
"Don't call me Andy."

"Andy, Andy," Betsy called again.
"Andy, there is a lion in this room."

"Look, Etsy, Etsy," I said.
"There is no lion in this room.
Go to sleep!"

That was all I said.
But Betsy began to cry.

"What is going on here?" my father said.

"Sandy called me Etsy," Betsy cried.
"And she said there was a lion
in this room.
And she said it was going to eat me up."

"I did not," I began to say.
But my father said,
"Sandy, don't say such a thing
to Betsy!
She is such a good girl."

Betsy was very quiet.
And then my father went out of the room.

Betsy got out of bed
and began to dance.
My father came back in the room.
"What is this?" he said.

"I had to dance," Betsy said.
"Sandy told me to!"

But this time my father said,
"Betsy, Sandy is in bed.
You are up and dancing.
Now, go to sleep."

Betsy got back in bed.
And that was that!

Part Three
Beets for Breakfast

At breakfast Betsy said, "I hate eggs.
I will not eat them."

My mother asked her
what she would eat for breakfast.

"Beets," Betsy said.

So Betsy ate beets for breakfast.
And I ate my eggs...all up.

Then Betsy wanted to play
the piano.
She played and played.
I wanted to play the piano, too.
So I played a little song.

But Betsy yelled,
"Stop it.
I hate that song.
That's a baby song."

But my father said,
"I like that song.
Play it again, Sandy."

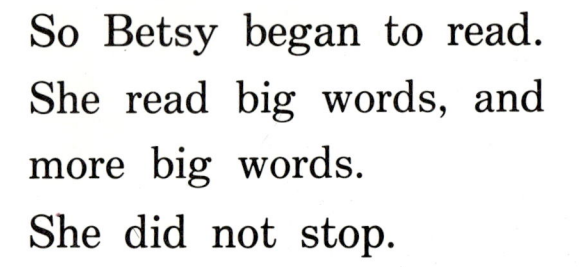

So Betsy began to read.
She read big words, and
more big words.
She did not stop.

I began to read a book I liked.
It had some big words, too.

Betsy yelled, "Stop it!
I hate that book!
That's a baby book!"

So I said,
"I like this book.
I think I'll read it again."

Then it was time to make our beds.

Betsy did not want to make her bed.
She did not want to play.

All she wanted to do was yell
about the things she didn't want to do.

So my mother said,
"What are we going to do with Betsy?"

And my father said,
"What are we going to do with Betsy?"

And I said,
"I know what to do with Betsy."

"Call her mother and tell her to take Betsy home!"

Everyone looked at me. Betsy was very quiet.

"I don't want to go home," she said at last. "I like it here. I want to stay."

My mother and father looked at Betsy and me.

"All right, Betsy," they said. "You can stay here if...

you can be more like Sandy."

So Betsy did stay with us.
She stayed with us for three days.

She ate eggs for breakfast.
We read books together.
We played the piano together.
And we made our beds.

We had a very good time.

I still don't always make my bed.
I still don't always eat my beets.
But now my mother never says it would be good for me to know Betsy.

THE END

Look What I Have!

"Look what I have!
Look what I have!
A licorice stick!"
Said little Bess
As I walked by.

So I said,
"Can I have a bite?
I'm your friend,
Aren't I, Bess?"

And Bess just looked
And ate it all up
And then she said, "Yes."

—Arnold Spilka

JUST AWFUL
Alma Whitney

Part One
How Do You Feel?

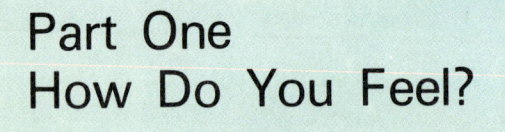

It was just after lunch
when James cut his finger
at the playground.

It hurt a little.
And it was bleeding, too.

James was feeling just awful.

He went to see his teacher.

"What is it, James?" she said.

"I cut my finger," said James.
"It is bleeding a little.
And it hurts, too."

"I see," said the teacher.
"How do you feel?"

"Just awful," said James.

"I think it would be good for you to see the nurse," said the teacher. "You can go right now."

James did not feel very happy. He had never gone to see the nurse.

James went into the nurse's room. He sat down next to a hurt foot and a runny nose.

The nurse called for the hurt foot.
The hurt foot went in to see her.
James stayed with the runny nose.

Then the hurt foot came out
of the nurse's room.
He looked very happy.

The nurse came out to the runny nose
and told her to come in.

James was all alone.
He did not feel good at all.

Then the runny nose came out.
And she looked very happy, too.

"Why couldn't I have a runny nose?"
thought James.
"Why do I have a cut finger?"

Then the nurse came to James.
She told James to come in.
He was feeling just awful.

Part Two
The Three-Part Treatment

James went in.
The nurse looked at his finger.

"How do you feel?" she asked.

"Just awful," said James.

The nurse looked at his finger again.
"I think you will be all right," she said.
"But I would like to give you
the three-part treatment."

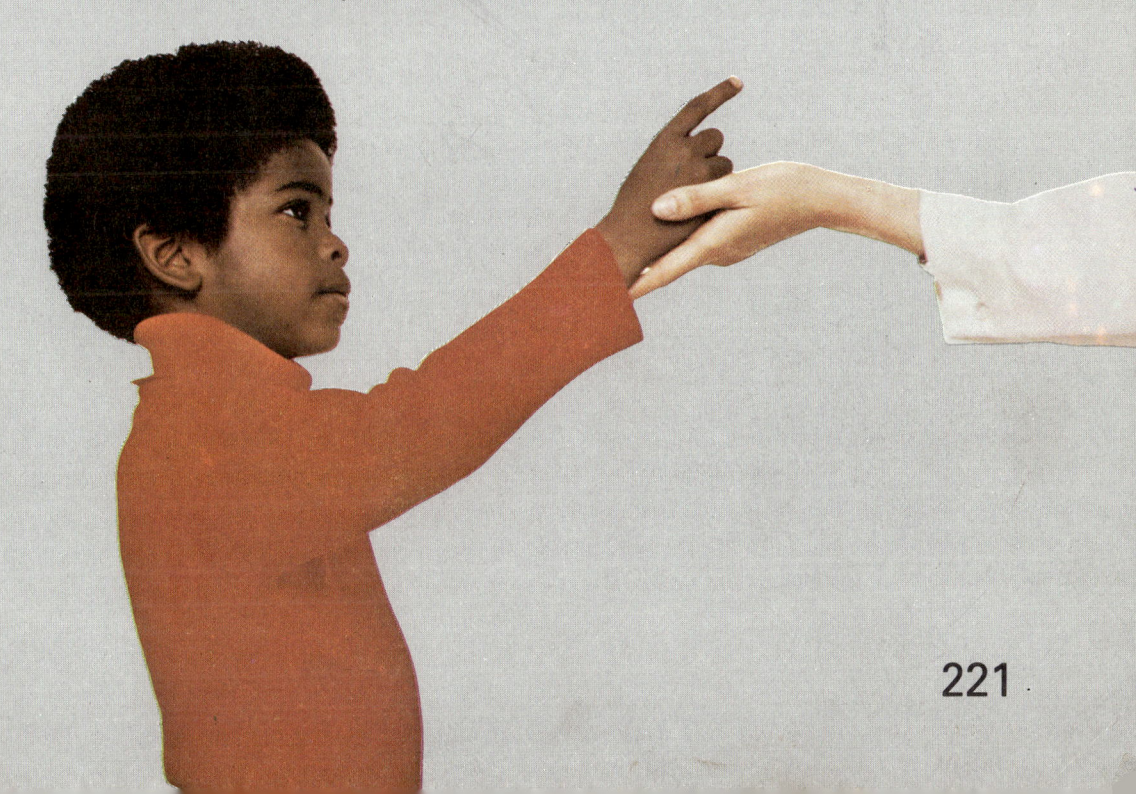

"The three-part treatment?" said James.
And he put his hands in back of him.
He had no idea what the nurse
was going to do.

"Yes, the three-part treatment,"
said the nurse.
"It will not be bad at all."

"This part is the cleaning," she said.
And she put his finger in some water.

The cleaning wasn't bad at all.
The finger didn't hurt.

Then the nurse took a little bandage out of a box.
"And now we will put a little bandage on your finger," she said.

Now things were not bad at all.
James liked the little bandage.
He began to feel good.

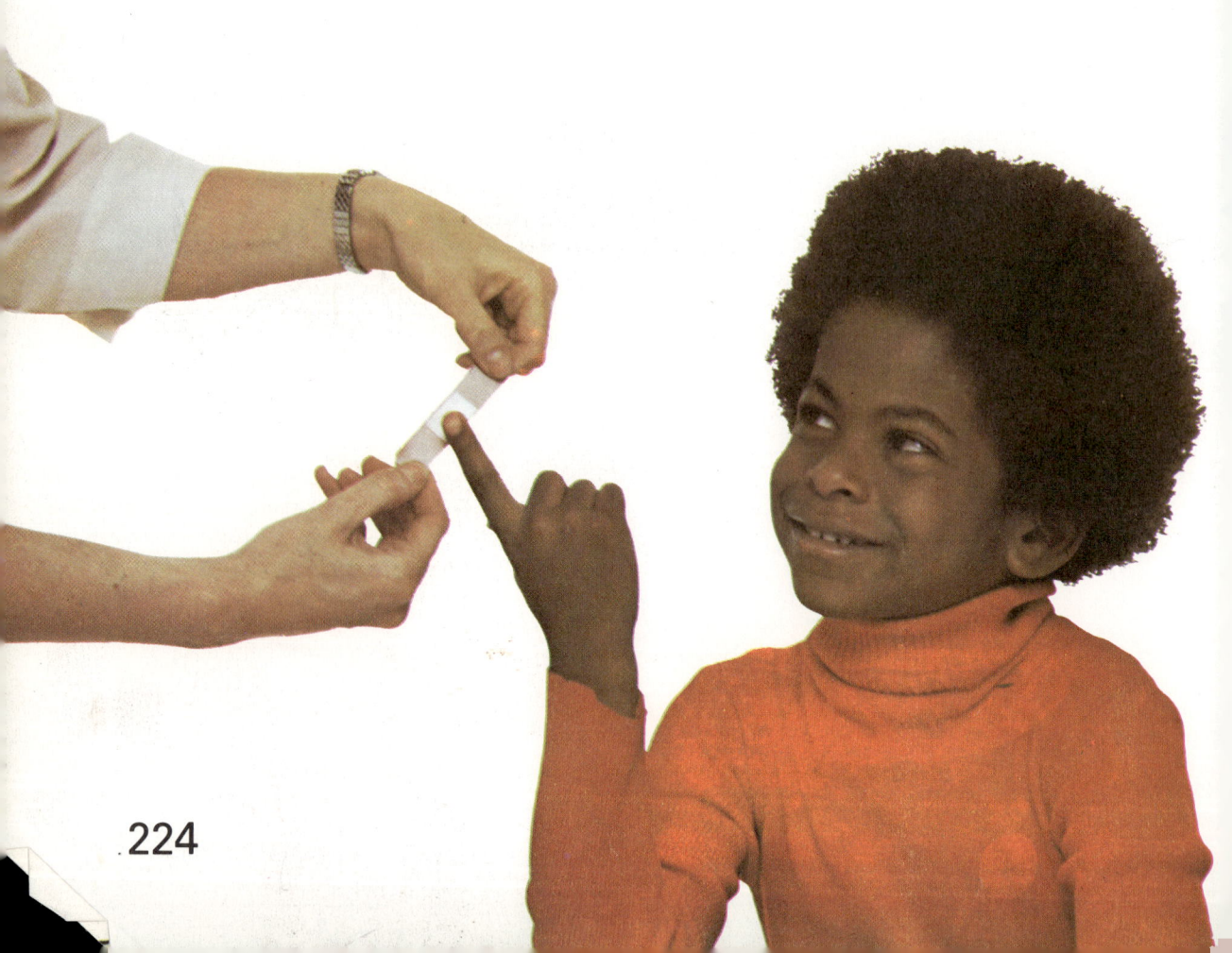

But then the nurse said,
"And now for the last part—
it is very important."

"Are you sure it is so important?"
said James.

"Yes, I'm sure," said the nurse.
"It is very important.
Now come here,
and I will give it to you."

James had no idea what would come next.
He began to feel awful again.

James walked very slowly to the nurse.

Just as he got to her, the nurse got up. She looked down at James and gave him a great big....

HUG!

James laughed a little.
"Boy," he said.
"I feel great!"

"Good," said the nurse.
"I think you can go back to your room now."

When James got back,
his teacher asked him how he was.

"I think I'll be all right now,"
said James.

You, whose day it is,
Make it beautiful.
Get out your rainbow colors,
So it will be beautiful.

—Nootka